CW00351173

RULE BRITANNIA

Also available:
The War Poets: an anthology

First published © Jarrold Publishing 1994
This reprint as *Rule Britannia: an anthology of patriotic poems*
© Pitkin Publishing 2009

Available through mail order. See our website,
www.pitkin-guides.com, for our full range of titles,
or contact us for a copy of our brochure.

Pitkin Publishing, Healey House, Dene Road,
Andover, Hampshire SP10 2AA
Sales and enquiries: 01264 409200
Fax: 01264 334110
Email: sales@thehistorypress.co.uk

ISBN: 978-1-84165-275-7   1/09

Printed in Singapore

CONTENTS

James Thomson (1700–48)

Rule Britannia 9

Michael Drayton (1563–1631)

Agincourt 11

William Shakespeare (1564–1616)

From: Henry V, Act III Scene I 18

Anonymous (c1600)

The 'Golden Vanity' 20

Jean Elliot (1727–1805)

Lament for Flodden 22

Sir Henry Newbolt (1862–1938)

Drake's Drum 24

Henry Austin Dobson (1840–1921)

A Ballad to Queen Elizabeth 26

Richard Lovelace (1618–57)

To Lucasta, on Going to the Wars 28

P.J. O'Reilly

Drake Goes West 29

Phoebe Cary

The Leak in the Dike 31

Robert Stephen Hawker (1803–75)

The Song of the Western Men 39

Robert Southey (1774–1843)

After Blenheim 41

Thomas Campbell (1777–1844)

Hohenlinden 45

Thomas Babington, Lord Macauley (1800–59)

A Jacobite's Epitaph 47

William Cowper (1731–1800)

Loss of the 'Royal George' 48

Charles Wolfe (1791–1823)

The Burial of Sir John Moore at Corunna 50

Sir Walter Scott (1771–1832)

Patriotism 52

Thomas Moore (1779–1852)

Pro Patria Mori 54

Thomas Campbell (1777–1844)

Ye Mariners of England 55

Alfred, Lord Tennyson (1809–92)

The Charge of the Heavy Brigade at Balaclava 57

The Charge of the Light Brigade 62

Sir Henry Newbolt (1862–1938)

Admirals All 65

The 'Old Superb' 68

Sir Francis Doyle (1810–88)

The Private of the Buffs 71

William Cory (1823–92)

A Ballad for a Boy 73

Thomas Campbell (1777–1844)

The Battle of the Baltic 79

John Whittier (1807–92)

Barbara Frietchie 82

Henry Lawson

Song of the Dardanelles 86

Said the Kaiser to the Spy 89

Fighting Hard 92

E.W. Tennant (1897–1916)

Home Thoughts in Laventie 95

W.N. Hodgson

Ave, Mater – Atque Vale *98*

John Freeman (1880–1929)

Happy is England Now *100*

George Robert Sims (1847–1922)

Won't You Join the Army? *102*

J.R. Wreford (1800–1881)

Lord, While for all Mankind we Pray *105*

Rupert Brooke (1887–1915)

The Soldier *106*

Laurence Binyon (1869–1943)

For the Fallen *107*

William Blake (1757–1827)

Jerusalem *109*

Robert Browning (1812–1889)

Home Thoughts, from Abroad *110*

Home Thoughts, from the Sea *111*

Sir Cecil Spring-Rice (1859–1918)

The Two Fatherlands *112*

William Henley (1849–1903)

England, My England *113*

Rudyard Kipling (1865–1936)

Land of our Birth 116

Fred E. Weatherly (1848–1929)

Up from Somerset 118

Neil Munro (1864–1930)

To Exiles 121

John Drinkwater (1882–1937)

The Midlands 124

Arthur Benson (1862–1925)

Land of Hope and Glory 127

JAMES THOMSON
RULE BRITANNIA

When Britain first at Heaven's command
  Arose from out the azure main,
This was the charter of her land,
  And guardian angels sung the strain:
Rule Britannia! Britannia rules the waves!
  Britons never shall be slaves.

The nations not so blest as thee
  Must in their turn to tyrants fall,
Whilst thou shalt flourish great and free
  The dread and envy of them all.

Still more majestic shalt thou rise,
  More dreadful from each foreign stroke;
As the loud blast that tears the skies
  Serves but to root thy native oak.

Thee haughty tyrants ne'er shall tame;
  All their attempts to bend thee down
Will but arouse thy generous flame,
  And work their woe and thy renown.

To thee belongs the rural reign;
    Thy cities shall with commerce shine;
All thine shall be the subject main,
    And every shore it circles thine!

The Muses, still with Freedom found,
    Shall to thy happy coast repair;
Blest Isle, with matchless beauty crown'd,
    And manly hearts to guard the fair: —
Rule Britannia! Britannia rules the waves!
    Britons never shall be slaves!

MICHAEL DRAYTON

AGINCOURT

Fair stood the wind for France
When we our sails advance,
Nor now to prove our chance
  Longer will tarry;
But putting to the main,
At Caux, the mouth of Seine,
With all his martial train
  Landed King Harry.

And taking many a fort,
Furnish'd in warlike sort,
Marcheth tow'rds Agincourt
  In happy hour;
Skirmishing day by day
With those that stopped his way,
Where the French gen'ral lay
  With all his power.

Which, in his height of pride,
King Henry to deride,
His ransom to provide
    Unto his sending;
Which he neglects the while
As from a nation vile,
Yet with an angry smile
    Their fall portending.

And turning to his men,
Quoth our brave Henry then,
"Though they to one be ten
    Be not amazèd:
Yet have we well begun;
Battles so bravely won
Have ever to the sun
    By fame been raisèd.

"And for myself (quoth he)
This my full rest shall be:
England ne'er mourn for me
    Nor more esteem me:

Victor I will remain
Or on this earth lie slain,
Never shall she sustain
    Loss to redeem me.

"Poitiers and Cressy tell,
When most their pride did swell,
Under our swords they fell:
    No less our skill is
Than when our grandsire great,
Claiming the regal seat,
By many a warlike feat
    Lopp'd the French lilies."

The Duke of York so dread
The eager vaward led;
With the main Henry sped
    Among his henchmen.
Excester had the rear,
A braver man not there;
O Lord, how hot they were
    On the false Frenchmen!

They now to fight are gone,
Armour on armour shone,
Drum now to drum did groan,
*   To hear was wonder;*
That with the cries they make
The very earth did shake:
Trumpet to trumpet spake,
*   Thunder to thunder.*

Well it thine age became,
O noble Erpingham,
Which didst the signal aim
*   To our hid forces!*
When from a meadow by,
Like a storm suddenly
The English archery
*   Struck the French horses.*

With Spanish yew so strong,
Arrows a cloth-yard long
That like to serpents stung,
*   Piercing the weather;*

None from his fellow starts,
But playing manly parts,
And like true English hearts
  Stuck close together.

When down their bows they threw,
And forth their bilbos drew,
And on the French they flew,
  Not one was tardy;
Arms were from shoulders sent,
Scalps to the teeth were rent,
Down the French peasants went –
  Our men were hardy.

This while our noble king,
His broadsword brandishing,
Down the French host did ding
  As to o'erwhelm it;
And many a deep wound lent,
His arms with blood besprent,
And many a cruel dent
  Bruisèd his helmet.

Gloster, that duke so good,
Next of the royal blood,
For famous England stood,
    With his brave brother;
Clarence, in steel so bright,
Though but a maiden knight,
Yet in that furious fight
    Scarce such another.

Warwick in blood did wade,
Oxford the foe invade,
And cruel slaughter made
    Still as they ran up;
Suffolk his axe did ply,
Beaumont and Willoughby
Bare them right doughtily,
    Ferrers and Fanhope.

Upon St Crispin's Day
Fought was this noble fray,
Which fame did not delay
    To England to carry.
O when shall Englishmen
With such acts fill a pen?
Or England breed again
    Such a King Harry?

WILLIAM SHAKESPEARE

FROM: HENRY V, ACT III SCENE I

KING HENRY:

Once more unto the breach, dear friends, once more;
Or close the wall up with our English dead!
In peace there's nothing so becomes a man
As modest stillness and humility:
But when the blast of war blows in our ears,
Then imitate the action of the tiger;
Stiffen the sinews, summon up the blood,
Disguise fair nature with hard-favour'd rage;
Then lend the eye a terrible aspect;
Let it pry through the portage of the head
Like the brass cannon; let the brow o 'erwhelm it
As fearfully as doth a galled rock
O'erhang and jutty his confounded base,
Swill'd with the wild and wasteful ocean.
Now set the teeth and stretch the nostril wide,
Hold hard the breath, and bend up every spirit
To his full height! On, on, you noblest English!
Whose blood is fet from fathers of war-proof;
Fathers that, like so many Alexanders,
Have in these parts from morn till even fought,

And sheath'd their swords for lack of argument.
Dishonour not your mothers; now attest
That those whom you called fathers did beget you.
Be copy now to men of grosser blood,
And teach them how to war. And you, good yeomen,
Whose limbs were made in England, show us here
The mettle of your pasture; let us swear
That you are worth your breeding; which I doubt not;
For there is none of you so mean and base
That hath not noble lustre in your eyes.
I see you stand like greyhounds in the slips,
Straining upon the start. The game's afoot:
Follow your spirit; and, upon this charge
Cry "God for Harry! England and Saint George!"

ANONYMOUS

THE 'GOLDEN VANITY'

A ship have I got in the North Countrie,
And she goes by the name of the 'Golden Vanitie';
O, I fear she will be taken by a Spanish Galalie,
*   As she sails by the Low-lands low.*

To the captain then up spake the little cabin-boy,
He said, "What is my fee if the galley I destroy?
The Spanish Galalie, if no more it shall annoy,
*   As you sail by the Low-lands low?"*

"Of silver and of gold I will give to you a store,
And my pretty little daughter that dwelleth on the
*   shore,*
Of treasure and of fee as well I'll give to thee galore,
*   As we sail by the Low-lands low."*

Then the boy bared his breast, and straightway leapèd
*   in,*
And he held in his hand an auger sharp and thin,
And he swam until he came to the Spanish galleon,
*   As she lay by the Low-lands low.*

He bored with the auger, he bored once and twice,
And some were playing cards, and some were playing
   dice;
When the water it flowed in, it dazzled their eyes,
   And she sank by the Low-lands low.

So the cabin-boy did swim all to the larboard side,
Saying, "Captain, take me in, I am drifting with the
   tide!"
"I will shoot you! I will kill you," the cruel captain
   cried,
   "You may sink by the Low-lands low."

Then the cabin-boy did swim all to the starboard side,
Saying, "Messmates, take me in, I am drifting with the
   tide!"
Then they laid him on the deck, and he closed his eyes
   and died,
   As they sailed by the Low-lands low.

They sewed his body up, all in an old cow's hide,
And they cast the gallant cabin-boy over the ship's side,
And left him without more ado a-drifting with the tide,
   And to sink by the Low-lands low.

Jean Elliott

Lament for Flodden

I've heard them lilting at our ewe-milking,
Lasses a' lilting before dawn o' day;
But now they are moaning on ilka green loaning —
The Flowers of the Forest are a' wede away.

At bughts, in the morning, nae blythe lads are scorning.
Lasses are lonely and dowie and wae;
Nae daffin', na gabbin', but sighing and sabbing,
Ilk ane lifts her leglin and hies her away.

In har'st, at the shearing, nae youths now are jeering,
Bandsters are lyart, and runkled, and gray;
At fair or at preaching, nae wooing, nae fleeching –
The Flowers of the Forest are a' wede away.

At e'en, in the gloaming, nae younkers are roaming
'Bout stacks wi' the lasses at bogle to play;
But ilk ane sits drearie, lamenting her dearie —
The Flowers of the Forest are weded away.

Dool and wae for the order, sent out lads to the
  Border!
The English, for ance, by guile wan the day;
The Flowers of the Forest, that fought aye the
  foremost,
The prime of our land, are cauld in the clay.

We'll hear nae mair lilting at the ewe-milking;
Women and bairns are heartless and wae;
Sighing and moaning on ilka green loaning –
The Flowers of the Forest are a' wede away.

SIR HENRY NEWBOLT

DRAKE'S DRUM

Drake he's in his hammock an' a thousand mile away,
(Capten, art tha sleepin' there below?)
Slung atween the round shot in Nombre Dios Bay,
An' dreamin' arl the time o' Plymouth Hoe.
Yarnder lumes the Island, yarnder lie the ships,
Wi' sailor lads a-dancin' heel-an'-toe,
An' the shore lights flashin', an' the night-tide dashin',
He sees et arl so plainly as he saw et long ago.

Drake he was a Devon man, an' ruled the Devon seas,
(Capten, art tha sleepin' there below?)
Rovin' tho' his death fell, he went wi' heart at ease,
An' dreamin' arl the time o' Plymouth Hoe.
"Take my drum to England, hang et by the shore,
Strike et when your powder's runnin' low;
If the Dons sight Devon, I'll quit the port o' Heaven
An' drum them up the Channel as we drumm'd them
*   long ago."*

Drake he's in his hammock till the great Armadas come,
(Capten, art tha sleepin' there below?),
Slung atween the round shot, listenin' for the drum,
An' dreamin' arl the time o' Plymouth Hoe.
Call him on the deep sea, call him up the Sound,
Call him when ye sail to meet the foe;
Where the old trade's plyin' an' the old flag flyin',
They shall find him ware an' wakin', as they found
    him long ago!

Henry Austin Dobson

A Ballad to Queen Elizabeth

King Philip had vaunted his claims;
*   He had sworn for a year he would sack us;*
With an army of heathenish names
*   He was coming to fagot and stack us*
*   Like the thieves of the sea he would track us,*
And shatter our ships on the main;
*   But we had bold Neptune to back us, –*
And where are the galleons of Spain?

His carackes were christened of dames
*   To the kirtles whereof he would tack us;*
With his saints and his gilded stern-frames,
*   He had thought like an egg-shell to crack us:*
*   How Howard may get to his Flaccus,*
And Drake to his Devon again,
*   And Hawkins bowl rubbers to Bacchus, –*
For where are the galleons of Spain?

Let his Majesty hang to St James
  The axe that he whetted to hack us;
He must play at some lustier games
  Or at sea he can hope to out-thwack us
  To his mines of Peru he would pack us
To tug at his bullet and chain;
  Alas! that his Greatness should lack us! –
But where are the galleons of Spain?

ENVOY

  Gloriana! the Don may attack us
Whenever his stomach be fain;
  He must reach us before he can rack us,
And where are the galleons of Spain?

Richard Lovelace

To Lucasta, on Going to the Wars

Tell me not, Sweet, I am unkind
That from the nunnery
Of thy chaste breast and quiet mind,
To war and arms I fly.

True, a new mistress now I chase,
The first foe in the field;
And with a stronger faith embrace
A sword, a horse, a shield.

Yet this inconstancy is such
As you too shall adore;
I could not love thee, Dear, so much,
Loved I not Honour more.

P.J. O'REILLY

DRAKE GOES WEST

Drake is going West, lad,
His ships are in the bay,
Five and twenty sail all told,
Ready for the fray!
Oh! hear it pass from lip to lip
"Drake is off again!"
Aye, Drake's away at break o' day,
To sweep the Spanish Main!
 Then here's to the Spanish Main —
 And here's to the foe!
 And here's to Drake and his merry, merry men,
 Who'll never come back to Devon again,
 Till they've laid the enemy low!

Drake is going West, lad,
You'd like to go, would you?
Then go you shall to share the fight
And the glory too!
Before our men the foe shall fall
Like the sickled grain,
For Drake is going Westward, lad,

To sweep the Spanish Main!
    Then here's to the Spanish Main —
    And here's to the foe!
    And here's to Drake and his merry, merry
        men,
    Who'll never come back to Devon again,
    Till they've laid the enemy low!

Some are going West, lad,
Who'll ne'er win home again —
Some will sleep their long, long sleep,
'Neath the Spanish Main!
But whatsoever be our fate —
Come what may, say I,
With Drake we'll go, for Drake we'll fight,
With Drake we'll win or die!
    Then here's to the Spanish Main —
    And here's to the foe!
    And here's to Drake and his merry, merry
        men,
    Who'll never come back to Devon again,
    Till they've laid the enemy low!

PHOEBE CARY

THE LEAK IN THE DIKE

The good dame looked from her cottage
At the close of a summer's day,
And cheerily called to her little son
Outside the door at play:
"Come, Peter, come! I want you to go,
While there is light to see,
To the hut of the blind old man who lives
Across the dike, for me;
And take these cakes I made for him, –
They are hot and smoking yet;
You have time enough to go and come
Before the sun is set."

Then the good wife turned to her labour,
Humming a simple song,
And thought of her husband, working hard
At the sluices all day long.
She set the turf a-blazing,
And brought the coarse black bread,
That he might find a fire at night,
And find the table spread.

And Peter left the brother,
With whom all day he had played,
And the sister who had watched their sports
In the willow's tender shade;
And told them they'd see him back before
They saw a star in sight,
Though he wouldn't be afraid to go
In the very darkest night!

For he was a brave, bright fellow,
With eye and conscience clear;
He could do whatever a boy might do,
And he had not learned to fear.
Why, he wouldn't have robbed a bird's nest,
Nor brought a stork to harm,
Though never a law in Holland
Had stood to stay his arm!

And now, with his face all glowing,
And eyes as bright as the day,
With the thoughts of his pleasant errand,
He trudged along the way;
And soon his joyous prattle
Made glad a lonesome place —

Ah! if only the blind old man
Could have seen that happy face!
Yet he somehow caught the brightness
Which Peter's presence lent;
And he felt the sunshine come and go
As Peter came and went.

And now, as the day was sinking,
And the winds began to rise,
The mother looked from her door again,
Shading her anxious eyes;
And saw the shadows deepen,
And birds to their homes come back,
But never a sign of Peter
Along the level track.
But she said: "He will come at morning,
So I need not fret or grieve, –
Though it isn't like my boy at all
To stay without my leave."

But where was the child delaying?
On the homeward way was he,
And across the dike while the sun was up
An hour above the sea.

He was stooping now to gather flowers,
Now listening to the sound,
As the angry waters dashed themselves
Against their narrow bound.
"Ah! well for us," said Peter,
"That the gates are good and strong,
And my father tends them carefully,
Or they would not hold you long!
You're a wicked, wicked, wicked sea;
I know why you fret and chafe;
You would like to spoil our lands and homes,
But our sluices keep you safe!"

But hark! through the noise of waters
Comes a low, clear, trickling sound;
And the child's face pales with terror,
And his blossoms drop to the ground.
He is up the bank in a moment,
And, stealing through the sand,
He sees a stream not yet so large
As his slender, childish hand.
'Tis a leak in the dike! He is but a boy,
Unused to fearful scenes;
But, young as he is, he has learned to know

The dreadful thing that means.
A leak in the dike! The stoutest heart
Grows faint that cry to hear,
And the bravest man in all the land
Turns white with mortal fear.
For he knows the smallest leak may grow
To a flood in a single night;
And he knows the strength of the cruel sea
When loosed in its angry might.

And the boy! he has seen the danger,
And, shouting a wild alarm,
He forces back the weight of the sea
With the strength of his single arm!
He listens for the joyful sound
Of a footstep passing nigh;
And lays his ear to the ground, to catch
An answer to his cry.
He hears the rough wind blowing,
And the waters rise and fall,
But never an answer comes to him,
Save the echo of his call.
He sees no hope, no succour —
His feeble voice is lost;

Yet what shall he do but watch and wait,
Though he perish at his post!

So, faintly calling and crying
Till the sun is under the sea;
Crying and moaning till the stars
Come out for company;
He thinks of his brother and sister,
Asleep in their safe warm bed;
He thinks of his father and mother,
Of himself as dying – and dead;
And of how, when the night is over,
They must come and find him at last;
But he never thinks he can leave the place
Where duty holds him fast.

The good dame in the cottage
Is up and astir with the light,
For the thought of her little Peter
Has been with her all night.
And now she watches the pathway,
As yester eve she had done;

But what does she see so strange and black
Against the rising sun?
Her neighbours are bearing between them
Something straight to her door –
The child is coming home, but not
As he ever came before!

"He is dead! – my boy – my darling!"
And the startled father hears,
And comes and looks the way she looks,
And fears the thing she fears;
Till a glad shout from the bearers
Thrills the stricken man and wife, –
"Give thanks; your son has saved our land,
And God has saved his life!"
So, there in the morning sunshine
They knelt about the boy;
And every head was bared and bent
In tearful, reverent joy.

'Tis many a year since then; but still,
When the sea roars like a flood,
Their boys are taught what a boy can do
Who is brave and true and good.
For every man in that country

Takes his son by the hand,
And tells him of little Peter,
Whose courage saved the land.

They have many a valiant hero
Remembered through the years,
But never one whose name so oft
Is named with loving tears.
And his deed shall be sung by the cradle,
And told to the child on the knee,
So long as the dikes of Holland
Divide the land from the sea!

Robert Stephen Hawker

The Song of the Western Men

A good sword and a trusty hand!
A merry heart and true!
King James's men shall understand
What Cornish lads can do.

And have they fixed the where and when?
And shall Trelawny die?
Here's twenty thousand Cornish men
Will know the reason why!

Out spake their captain brave and bold,
A merry wight was he:
"If London Tower were Michael's hold,
We'll set Trelawny free!

"We'll cross the Tamar, land to land,
The Severn is no stay,
With 'one and all', and hand in hand,
And who shall bid us nay?

"And when we come to London Wall,
A pleasant sight to view,
Come forth! come forth, ye cowards all,
Here's men as good as you.

"Trelawny he's in keep and hold,
Trelawny he may die;
But here's twenty thousand Cornish bold
Will know the reason why!"

ROBERT SOUTHEY

AFTER BLENHEIM

It was a summer evening,
Old Kaspar's work was done,
And he before his cottage door
Was sitting in the sun;
And by him sported on the green
His little grandchild Wilhelmine.

She saw her brother Peterkin
Roll something large and round
Which he beside the rivulet
In playing there had found;
He came to ask what he had found
That was so large and smooth and round.

Old Kaspar took it from the boy
Who stood expectant by;
And then the old man shook his head,
And with a natural sigh
"'Tis some poor fellow's skull," said he,
"Who fell in the great victory.

"I find them in the garden,
For there's many here about;
And often when I go to plough
The ploughshare turns them out.
For many thousand men," said he,
"Were slain in that great victory."

"Now tell us what 'twas all about,"
Young Peterkin he cries;
And little Wilhelmine looks up
With wonder-waiting eyes;
"Now tell us all about the war,
And what they fought each other for."

"It was the English," Kaspar cried,
"Who put the French to rout;
But what they fought each other for
I could not well make out.
But everybody said," quoth he,
"That 'twas a famous victory.

"My father lived at Blenheim then,
Yon little stream hard by;
They burnt his dwelling to the ground,
And he was forced to fly:
So with his wife and child he fled,
Nor had he where to rest his head.

"With fire and sword the country round
Was wasted far and wide,
And many a childing mother then
And new-born baby died:
But things like that, you know, must be
At every famous victory.

"They say it was a shocking sight
After the field was won;
For many thousand bodies here
Lay rotting in the sun:
But things like that, you know, must be
After a famous victory.

"Great praise the Duke of Marlbro' won
And our good Prince Eugene;"
"Why, 'twas a very wicked thing!"
Said little Wilhelmine;
"Nay . . nay . . my little girl," quoth he,
"It was a famous victory.

"And everybody praised the Duke
Who this great fight did win."
"But what good came of it at last?"
Quoth little Peterkin: –
"Why, that I cannot tell," said he,
"But 'twas a famous victory."

Thomas Campbell

Hohenlinden

On Linden, when the sun was low,
All bloodless lay the untrodden snow;
And dark as winter was the flow
    Of Iser, rolling rapidly.

But Linden saw another sight,
When the drum beat at dead of night,
Commanding fires of death to light
    The darkness of her scenery.

By torch and trumpet fast array'd
Each horseman drew his battle blade
And furious every charger neigh'd
    To join the dreadful revelry.

Then shook the hills with thunder riven,
Then rush'd the steed, to battle driven,
And louder than the bolts of Heaven
    Far flash'd the red artillery.

But redder yet that light shall glow
On Linden's hills of stained snow;
And bloodier yet the torrent flow
    Of Iser, rolling rapidly.

'Tis morn; but scarce yon level sun
Can pierce the war-clouds, rolling dun,
Where furious Frank and fiery Hun
    Shout in their sulphurous canopy.

The combat deepens. On, ye brave
Who rush to glory, or the grave!
Wave, Munich, all thy banners wave,
    And charge with all thy chivalry!

Few, few shall part, where many meet!
The snow shall be their winding-sheet,
And every turf beneath their feet
    Shall be a soldier's sepulchre.

Thomas Babington, Lord Macaulay

A Jacobite's Epitaph

To my true king I offered free from stain
Courage and faith; vain faith, and courage vain.
For him I threw lands, honours, wealth, away,
And one dear hope, that was more prized then they.
For him I languished in a foreign clime,
Grey-haired with sorrow in my manhood's prime;
Heard on Lavernia Scargill's whispering trees,
And pined by Arno for my lovelier Tees;
Beheld each night my home in fevered sleep,
Each morning started from the dream to weep;
Till God, who saw me tried too sorely, gave
The resting-place I asked, an early grave.
O thou, whom chance leads to this nameless stone,
From that proud country which was once mine own,
By those white cliffs I never more must see,
By that dear language which I spake like thee,
Forget all feuds, and shed one English tear.
O'er English dust. A broken heart lies here.

WILLIAM COWPER

LOSS OF THE 'ROYAL GEORGE'

Toll for the Brave!
The brave that are no more!
All sunk beneath the wave
Fast by their native shore!

Eight hundred of the brave,
Whose courage well was tried,
Had made the vessel heel
And laid her on her side.

A land-breeze shook the shrouds
And she was overset;
Down went the 'Royal George',
With all her crew complete.

Toll for the brave!
Brave Kempenfelt is gone:
His last sea-fight is fought,
His work of glory done.

It was not in the battle;
No tempest gave the shock;
She sprang no fatal leak,
She ran upon no rock.

His sword was in the sheath,
His fingers held the pen,
When Kempenfelt went down
With twice four hundred men.

Weigh the vessel up
Once dreaded by our foes,
And mingle with your cup
The tears that England owes.

Her timbers yet are sound,
And she may float again
Full charged with England's thunder,
And plough the distant main:

But Kempenfelt is gone,
His victories are o'er;
And he and his eight hundred
Must plough the wave no more.

CHARLES WOLFE

THE BURIAL OF SIR JOHN MOORE AT CORUNNA

Not a drum was heard, not a funeral note,
As his corse to the rampart we hurried;
Not a soldier discharged his farewell shot
O'er the grave where our Hero we buried.

We buried him darkly at dead of night,
The sods with our bayonets turning;
By the struggling moonbeam's misty light
And the lantern dimly burning.

No useless coffin enclosed his breast,
Not in sheet or in shroud we wound him;
But he lay like a Warrior taking his rest
With his martial cloak around him.

Few and short were the prayers we said,
And we spoke not a word of sorrow;
But we steadfastly gaz'd on the face that was dead,
And we bitterly thought of the morrow.

We thought, as we hollow'd his narrow bed
And smooth'd down his lonely pillow,
That the Foe and the Stranger would tread o'er
   his head,
And we far away on the billow!

Lightly they'll talk of the Spirit that's gone
And o'er his cold ashes upbraid him, —
But little he'll reck, if they let him sleep on
In the grave where a Briton has laid him.

But half of our heavy task was done
When the clock struck the hour for retiring:
And we heard the distant and random gun
That the foe was sullenly firing.

Slowly and sadly we laid him down,
From the field of his fame fresh and gory;
We carved not a line, and we raised not a stone —
But we left him alone with his glory.

Sir Walter Scott

Patriotism

I

Breathes there the man, with soul so dead,
Who never to himself hath said,
   This is my own, my native land!
Whose heart hath ne'er within him burned,
As home his footsteps he hath turned,
   From wandering on a foreign strand!
If such there breathe, go, mark him well;
For him no Minstrel raptures swell;
High though his titles, proud his name,
Boundless his wealth as wish can claim;
Despite those titles, power, and pelf,
The wretch, concentred all in self,
Living, shall forfeit fair renown,
And, doubly dying, shall go down
To the vile dust, from whence he sprung,
Unwept, unhonoured, and unsung.

II

O Caledonia! stern and wild,
Meet nurse for a poetic child!
Land of brown heath and shaggy wood,
Land of the mountain and the flood,
Land of my sires! what mortal hand
Can e'er untie the filial band,
That knits me to thy rugged strand!
Still as I view each well-known scene,
Think what is now, and what hath been,
Seems as, to me, of all bereft,
Sole friends thy woods and streams were left;
And thus I love them better still,
Even in extremity of ill.
By Yarrow's stream still let me stray,
Though none should guide my feeble way;
Still feel the breeze down Ettrick break,
Although it chill my withered cheek;
Still lay my head by Teviot Stone,
Though there, forgotten and alone,
The Bard may draw his parting groan.

Thomas Moore

Pro Patria Mori

When he who adores thee has left but the name
Of his fault and his sorrows behind,
O! say wilt thou weep, when they darken the fame
Of a life that for thee was resigned?
Yes, weep, and however my foes may condemn,
Thy tears shall efface their decree;
For, Heaven can witness, though guilty to them,
I have been but too faithful to thee.

With thee were the dreams of my earliest love,
Every thought of my reason was thine:
In my last humble prayer to the Spirit above
Thy name shall be mingled with mine!
O! blest are the lovers and friends who shall live
The days of thy glory to see;
But the next dearest blessing that Heaven can give
Is the pride of thus dying for thee.

Thomas Campbell

Ye Mariners of England

Ye Mariners of England
That guard our native seas,
Whose flag has braved, a thousand years,
The battle and the breeze,
Your glorious standard launch again
To match another foe:
And sweep through the deep,
While the stormy winds do blow;
While the battle rages loud and long
And the stormy winds do blow.

The spirits of your fathers
Shall start from every wave —
For the deck it was their field of fame,
And Ocean was their grave.
Where Blake and mighty Nelson fell
Your manly hearts shall glow,
As ye sweep through the deep,
While the stormy winds do blow;
While the battle rages loud and long
And the stormy winds do blow.

Britannia needs no bulwarks,
No towers along the steep;
Her march is o'er the mountain waves,
Her home is on the deep.
With thunders from her native oak
She quells the floods below –
As they roar on the shore,
When the stormy winds do blow;
When the battle rages loud and long,
And the stormy winds do blow.

The meteor flag of England
Shall yet terrific burn;
Till danger's troubled night depart
And the star of peace return.
Then, then, ye ocean warriors!
Our song and feast shall flow
To the fame of your name,
When the storm has ceased to blow;
When the fiery fight is heard no more,
And the storm has ceased to blow.

Alfred, Lord Tennyson

The Charge of the Heavy Brigade at Balaclava

The charge of the gallant three hundred,
  the Heavy Brigade!
Down the hill, down the hill, thousands
  of Russians,
Thousands of horsemen, drew to the
  valley — and stay'd;
For Scarlett and Scarlett's three hundred
  were riding by
When the points of the Russian lances
  arose in the sky;
And he call'd "Left wheel into line!"
  and they wheel'd and obey'd.
Then he look'd at the host that had
  halted he knew not why,
And he turn'd half round, and he bad his
  trumpeter sound
To the charge, and he rode on ahead, as
  he waved his blade

To the gallant three hundred whose glory
   will never die –
"Follow," and up the hill, up the hill,
   up the hill,
Follow'd the Heavy Brigade.

The trumpet, the gallop, the charge,
   and the might of the fight!
Thousands of horsemen had gather'd
   there on the height,
With a wing push'd out to the left and
   a wing to the right,
And who shall escape if they close? but
   he dash'd up alone
Thro' the great grey slope of men,
Sway'd his sabre, and held his own
Like an Englishman there and then;
All in a moment follow'd with force
Three that were next in their fiery
   course,
Wedged themselves in between horse
   and horse,
Fought for their lives in the narrow gap
   they had made –

Four amid thousands! and up the hill,
  up the hill,
Gallopt the gallant three hundred, the
  Heavy Brigade.

Fell like a cannonshot,
Burst like a thunderbolt,
Crash'd like a hurricane,
Broke thro' the mass from below,
Drove thro' the midst of the foe,
Plunged up and down, to and fro,
Rode flashing blow upon blow,
Brave Inniskillens and Greys
Whirling their sabres in circles of light!
And some of us, all in amaze,
Who were held for a while from the
  fight,
And were only standing at gaze,
When the dark-muffled Russian crowd
Folded its wings from the left and the
  right,
And roll'd them around like a cloud, —
O mad for the charge and the battle
  were we,

When our own good redcoats sank from
    sight,
Like drops of blood in a dark-grey sea,
And we turn'd to each other, whispering,
    all dismay'd,
"Lost are the gallant three hundred of
    Scarlett's Brigade!"

"Lost one and all" were the words
Mutter'd in our dismay;
But they rode like Victors and Lords
Thro' the forest of lances and swords
In the heart of the Russian hordes,
They rode, or they stood at bay –
Struck with the sword-hand and slew,
Down with the bridle-hand drew
The foe from the saddle and threw
Underfoot there in the fray –
Ranged like a storm or stood like a rock
In the wave of a stormy day;
Till suddenly shock upon shock
Stagger'd the mass from without,
Drove it in wild disarray,

For our men gallopt up with a cheer and
    a shout,
And the foeman surged, and waver'd, and
    reel'd
Up the hill, up the hill, up the hill, out
    of the field,
And over the brow and away.

Glory to each and to all, and the charge
    that they made!
Glory to all the three hundred, and all
    the Brigade!

ALFRED, LORD TENNYSON

THE CHARGE OF THE LIGHT BRIGADE

Half a league, half a league,
   Half a league onward,
All in the valley of Death
   Rode the six hundred.
"Forward, the Light Brigade!
Charge for the guns!" he said:
Into the valley of Death
   Rode the six hundred.

"Forward, the Light Brigade!"
Was there a man dismay'd?
Not tho' the soldier knew
   Some one had blunder'd:
Their's not to make reply,
Their's not to reason why,
Their's but to do and die:
Into the valley of Death
   Rode the six hundred:

Cannon to right of them,
Cannon to left of them,
Cannon in front of them
    Volley'd and thunder'd;
Storm'd at with shot and shell,
Boldly they rode and well,
Into the jaws of Death,
Into the mouth of Hell
    Rode the six hundred.

Flash'd all their sabres bare,
Flash'd as they turn'd in air
Sabring the gunners there,
Charging an army, while
    All the world wonder'd:
Plunged in the battery-smoke
Right thro' the line they broke;
Cossack and Russian
Reel'd from the sabre-stroke
    Shatter'd and sunder'd.
Then they rode back, but not
    Not the six hundred.

Cannon to right of them,
Cannon to left of them,
Cannon behind them
    Volley'd and thunder'd;
Storm'd at with shot and shell,
While horse and hero fell,
They that had fought so well
Came thro' the jaws of Death,
Back from the mouth of Hell,
All that was left of them,
    Left of six hundred.

When can their glory fade?
O the wild charge they made!
    All the world wonder'd.
Honour the charge they made!
Honour the Light Brigade,
    Noble six hundred!

Sir Henry Newbolt

Admirals All

Effingham, Grenville, Raleigh, Drake,
Here's to the bold and free!
Benbow, Collingwood, Byron, Blake,
Hail to the Kings of the Sea!
Admirals all, for England's sake,
Honour be yours and fame!
And honour, as long as waves shall break,
To Nelson's peerlees name!
Admirals all, for England's sake,
Honour be yours and fame!
And honour, as long as waves shall break,
To Nelson's peerless name!

Essex was fretting in Cadiz Bay
With the galleons fair in sight;
Howard at last must give him his way,
And the word was passed to fight.
Never was schoolboy gayer than he,
Since holidays first began:
He tossed his bonnet to wind and sea,
And under the guns he ran.

Drake nor devil nor Spaniard feared,
Their cities he put to the sack;
He singed His Catholic Majesty's beard,
And harried his ships to wrack.
He was playing at Plymouth a rubber of bowls
When the great Armada came;
But he said, "They must wait their turn, good souls,"
And he stooped, and finished the game.

Fifteen sail were the Dutchmen bold,
Duncan he had but two;
But he anchored them fast where the Texel shoaled
And his colours aloft he flew.
"I've taken the depth to a fathom," he cried,
"An I'll sink with a right good will,
For I know when we're all of us under the tide
My flag will be fluttering still."

Splinters were flying above, below,
When Nelson sailed the Sound:
"Mark you, I wouldn't be elsewhere now,"
Said he, "for a thousand pound!"
The Admiral's signal bade him fly,
But he wickedly wagged his head,

He clapped the glass to his sightless eye,
And "I'm damned if I see it!" he said.

Admirals all, they said their say
(The echoes are ringing still),
Admirals all, they went their way
To the haven under the hill.
But they left us a kingdom none can take,
The realm of the circling sea,
To be ruled by the rightful sons of Blake
And the Rodneys yet to be.
Admirals all, for England's sake,
Honour be yours and fame!
And honour as long as waves shall break,
To Nelson's peerless name!

SIR HENRY NEWBOLT

THE 'OLD SUPERB'

The wind was rising easterly, the morning sky was blue,
The Straits before us open'd wide and free;
We look'd towards the Admiral, where high the Peter
  flew,
And all our hearts were dancing like the sea.
The French are gone to Martinique with four and twenty
  sail,
The 'Old Superb' is old and foul and slow;
But the French are gone to Martinique, and Nelson's on
  the trail,
And where he goes the 'Old Superb' must go.
  So Westward ho! for Trinidad, and Eastward ho!
    for Spain,
  And 'Ship a-hoy!' a hundred times a day;
  Round the world if need be, and round the
    world again
  With a lame duck lagging, lagging all the way.

The 'Old Superb' was barnacled and green as grass
  below,
Her sticks were only fit for stirring grog;

The pride of all her midshipmen was silent long ago,
And long ago they ceased to heave the log,
Four year out from home she was, and ne'er a week in
*   port,*
And nothing save the guns aboard her bright;
But Captain Keats he knew the game, and swore to share
*   the sport,*
For he never yet came in too late to fight.
*   So Westward ho! for Trinidad, and Eastward ho!*
*   for Spain,*
*   And 'Ship a-hoy!' a hundred times a day;*
*   Round the world if need be, and round the*
*   world again*
*   With a lame duck lagging, lagging all the way.*

"Now up, my lads," the Captain cried, "for sure the case
*   were hard*
If longest out were first to fall behind;
Aloft, aloft with studding sails, and lash them on the
*   yard,*
For night and day the trades are driving blind."
So all day long and all day long behind the fleet we crept,
And how we fretted none but Nelson guessed;

But ev'ry night the 'Old Superb' she sail'd when others
  slept,
Till we ran the French to earth with all the rest.
    O 'twas Westward ho! for Trinidad, and
      Eastward ho! for Spain,
    And 'Ship a-hoy!' a hundred times a day;
    Round the world if need be, and round the
      world again,
    With a lame duck, a lame duck a-lagging,
      lagging, lagging all the way!

SIR FRANCIS DOYLE

THE PRIVATE OF THE BUFFS

Last night, *among his fellow roughs,*
He jested, quaffed, and swore,
A drunken private of the Buffs,
Who never looked before.
To-day, beneath the foeman's frown,
He stands in Elgin's place,
Ambassador from Britain's crown,
And type of all her race.

Poor, reckless, rude, low-born, untaught,
Bewildered, and alone,
A heart, with English instinct fraught,
He yet can call his own.
Aye, tear his body limb from limb,
Bring cord, or axe, or flame:
He only knows, that not through him
Shall England come to shame.

Far Kentish hop-fields round him seem'd,
Like dreams, to come and go;
Bright leagues of cherry-blossom gleam'd,

One sheet of living snow;
The smoke, above his father's door,
In grey soft eddyings hung:
Must he then watch it rise no more,
Doom'd by himself so young?

Yes, honour calls! – with strength like steel
He put the vision by.
Let dusky Indians whine and kneel;
An English lad must die.
And thus, with eyes that would not shrink,
With knee to man unbent,
Unfaltering on its dreadful brink,
To his red grave he went.

Vain, mightiest fleets of iron framed;
Vain, those all-shattering guns;
Unless proud England keep, untamed,
The strong heart of her sons.
So, let his name through Europe ring –
A man of mean estate,
Who died, as firm as Sparta's King,
Because his soul was great.

WILLIAM CORY

A BALLAD FOR A BOY

When George III was reigning a hundred years ago,
He ordered Captain Farmer to chase the foreign foe.
"You're not afraid of shot," said he, "you're not afraid of
  wreck,
So cruise about the west of France in the Frigate called
  Quebec.

"Quebec was once a Frenchman's town, but twenty years
  ago
King George the Second sent a man called General
  Wolfe, you know,
To clamber up a precipice and look into Quebec
As you'd look down a hatchway when standing on the
  deck.

"If Wolfe could beat the Frenchmen then, so you can beat
  them now,
Before he got inside the town he died, I must allow.
But since the town was won for us, it is a lucky name,
And you'll remember Wolfe's good work, and you shall
  do the same."

Then Farmer said, "I'll try, sir," and Farmer bowed so
  low
That George could see his pig-tail tied in a velvet bow.
George gave him his commission, and that it might be
  safer,
Signed "King of Britain, King of France," and sealed it
  with a wafer.

Then proud was Captain Farmer in a frigate of his own.
And grander on his quarter-deck than George upon his
  throne.
He'd two guns in his cabin, and on the spar-deck ten,
And twenty on the gun-deck, and more than ten score
  men.

And as a huntsman scours the brakes with sixteen brace
  of dogs,
With two and thirty cannon the ship explored the fogs.
From Cape la Hogue to Ushant, from Rochefort to
  Belleisle,
She hunted game till reef and mud were rubbing on her
  keel.

The fogs are dried. The frigate's side is bright with
  melting tar.
The lad up in the foretop sees square white sails afar.
The east wind drives three square-sailed masts from out
  the Breton bay,
And "Clear for action!" Farmer shouts, and reefers yell
  "Hooray!"

The Frenchmen's captain had a name I wish I could
  pronounce.
A Breton gentleman was he, and wholly free from
  bounce,
One like those famous fellows who died by guillotine
For honour and the fleur de lys and Antoinette the
  Queen.

The Catholic for Louis, the Protestant for George,
Each captain drew as bright a sword as saintly smiths
  could forge:
And both were simple seamen, but both could understand
How each was bound to win or die for flag and native
  land.

The French ship was 'La Surveillante', which means the
  'Watchful Maid';
She folded up her head-dress and began her cannonade.
Her hull was clean and ours was foul; we had to spread
  more sail.
On canvas, stays, and topsail yards her bullets came like
  hail.

Sore smitten were both captains, and many lads beside,
And still to cut our rigging the foreign gunners tried.
A sail-clad spar came flapping down athwart a blazing
  gun;
We could not quench the rushing flames, and so the
  Frenchman won.

Our quarter deck was crowded; the waist was all aglow;
Men hung upon the taffrail, half scorched but loth to go;
Our captain sat where once we stood and would not quit
  his chair,
He bade his comrades leap for life, and leave him bleeding
  there.

The guns were hushed on either side. The Frenchmen
  lowered boats.
They flung us planks and hen-coops, and everything that
  floats.
They risked their lives, good fellows, to bring their rivals
  aid!
'Twas by the conflagration the peace was strangely made.

'La Surveillante' was like a sieve; the victors had no rest.
They had to dodge the East wind to reach the port of
  Brest,
And where the waves leapt power, and the riddled ship
  went slower,
In triumph, yet in funeral guise, came fisherboats to tow
  her.

They dealt with us as brethren, they mourned for Farmer
  dead;
And as each wounded captive passed each Breton bowed
  the head.

Then spoke the French lieutenant, "'Twas fire that won,
   not we.
You never struck your flag to us; you'll go to England
   free."
'Twas the sixth day of October, seventeen hundred
   seventy-nine,
A year when nations ventured against us to combine,
Quebec was burnt and Farmer slain, by us remembered
   not;
But thanks be to the French book wherein they're not
   forgot.

Now you, if you've to fight the French, my youngster,
   bear in mind
Those seamen of King Louis so chivalrous and kind;
Think of the Breton gentlemen who took our lads to
   Brest,
And treat some rescued Breton as a comrade and a guest.

Thomas Campbell

The Battle of the Baltic

Of Nelson and the North
Sing the glorious day's renown,
When to battle fierce came forth
All the might of Denmark's crown.
And her arms along the deep proudly shone;
By each gun the lighted brand
In a bold determined hand,
And the Prince of all the land
Led them on.

Like leviathans afloat,
Lay their bulwarks on the brine;
While the sign of battle flew
On the lofty British line:
It was ten of April morn by the chime:
As they drifted on their path,
There was silence deep as death;
And the boldest held his breath,
For a time.

But the might of England flushed
To anticipate the scene;
And her van the fleeter rushed
O'er the deadly space between.
"Hearts of oak!" our captains cried; when each
    gun
From its adamantine lips
Spread a death-shade round the ships,
Like the hurricane eclipse
Of the sun.

Again! again! again!
And the havoc did not slack,
Till a feeble cheer the Dane
To our cheering sent us back; –
Their shots along the deep slowly boom; –
Then ceased, and all is wail,
As they strike the shattered sail;
Or, in conflagration pale,
Light the gloom.

Out spoke the victor then,
As he hailed them o'er the wave:
"Ye are brothers! ye are men!
And we conquer but to save;
So peace instead of death let us bring.
But yield, proud foe, thy fleet
With the crews, at England's feet,
And make submission meet
To our King."

Now joy, Old England, raise
For the tidings of thy might,
By the festal cities' blaze,
While the wine-cup shines in light;
And yet amidst that joy and uproar,
Let us think of them that sleep
Full many a fathom deep
By thy wild and stormy steep,
Elsinore!

JOHN WHITTIER

BARBARA FRIETCHIE

Up from the meadows rich with corn
Clear in the cool September morn,

The clustered spires of Frederick stand
Green-walled by the hills of Maryland.

Round about them orchards sweep,
Apple and peach-tree fruited deep;

Fair as a garden of the Lord
To the eyes of the famished rebel horde.

On that pleasant morn of the early fall,
When Lee marched over the mountain wall –

Over the mountains winding down,
Horse and foot, into Frederick town.

Forty flags with their silver stars,
Forty flags with their crimson bars,

Flapped in the morning wind: the sun
Of noon looked down, and saw not one.

Up rose old Barbara Frietchie then,
Bowed with her fourscore years and ten;

Bravest of all in Frederick town,
She took up the flag the men hauled down;

In her attic-window the staff she set,
To show that one heart was loyal yet.

Up the street came the rebel tread,
Stonewall Jackson riding ahead.

Under his slouched hat left and right
He glanced; the old flag met his sight.

"Halt!" – the dust-brown ranks stood fast.
"Fire!" – out blazed the rifle-blast.

It shivered the window, pane and sash;
It rent the banner with seam and gash.

Quick, as it fell from the broken staff,
Dame Barbara snatched the silken scarf;

She leaned far out on the window-sill,
And shook it forth with a royal will.

"Shoot, if you must, this old grey head,
But spare your country's flag," she said.

A shade of sadness, a blush of shame,
Over the face of the leader came;

The nobler nature within him stirred
To life at that woman's deed and word:

"Who touches a hair of yon grey head
Dies like a dog. March on!" he said.

Al day long through Frederick street
Sounded the tread of marching feet

All day long that free flag tost
Over the heads of the rebel host.

Ever its torn folds rose and fell
On the loyal winds that loved it well;

And through the hill-gaps sunset light
Shone over it with a warm good-night.

Barbara Frietchie's work is o'er,
And the rebel rides on his raids no more.

Honour to her! and let a tear
Fall, for her sake, on Stonewall's bier.

Over Barbara Frietchie's grave,
Flag of Freedom and Union, wave!

Peace and order and beauty draw
Round thy symbol of light and law;

And ever the stars above look down
On thy stars below in Frederick town!

Henry Lawson

Song of the Dardanelles

The wireless tells and the cable tells
How our boys behaved by the Dardanelles.
Some thought in their hearts "Will our boys make
    good?"
We knew them of old and we knew they would!
    Knew they would –
    Knew they would;
We were mates of old and we knew they would.

They laughed and they larked and they loved likewise,
For blood is warm under Southern skies;
They knew not Pharaoh ('tis understood),
And they got into scrapes, as we knew they would.
    Knew they would –
    Knew they would;
And they got into scrapes, as we knew they would

They chafed in the dust of an old dead land
At the long months' drill in the scorching sand;
But they knew in their hearts it was for their good,
And they saw it through as we knew they would.

Knew they would –
Knew they would;
And they saw it through as we knew they would

The Coo-ee called through the Mena Camp,
And an army roared like the Ocean's tramp
On a gale-swept beach in her wildest mood,
Till the Pyramids shook as we knew they would
Knew they would –
Knew they would.
(And the Sphinx woke up as we knew she would.)

They were shipped like sheep when the dawn was grey;
(But their officers knew that no lambs were they).
They squatted and perched where'er they could,
And they 'blanky-ed' for joy as we knew they would
Knew they would –
Knew they would;
They 'blanky-ed' for joy as we knew they would.

The sea was hell and the shore was hell,
With mine, entanglement, shrapnel and shell,
But they stormed the heights as Australians should,
And they fought and they died as we knew they would.

Knew they would –
Knew they would;
They fought and they died as we knew they would.

From the southern hills and the city lanes,
From the sandwaste lone and the Blacksoil Plains;
The youngest and strongest of England's brood! –
They'll win for the South as we knew they would.
Knew they would –
Knew they would;
They'll win for the South as we knew they would.

HENRY LAWSON

SAID THE KAISER TO THE SPY

"Now tell me what can England do?"
    Said the Kaiser to the Spy.
"She can do nought, your Majesty –
    You rule the sea and sky.
Her day of destiny is done;
    Her path of peace is plain;
For she dare never throw a troop
    Across the Strait again."

The Kaiser sent his mighty host,
    With Bombast in advance,
To set his seal on Paris first,
    And make an end of France.
Their guns were heard in Paris streets,
    And trembling Europe heard;
(They're staggering back in Belgium now)
    And England said no word.

"Now tell me what can England do?"
    Said the Kaiser to the Spy.
"She can do nought in Southern seas

Where her possessions lie!
Her colonies are arming now –
    They only wait your aid!"
"I'll send my ships," the Kaiser said,
    "And I will kill her trade!"

The Kaiser sent his cruisers forth
    To do their worst or best;
And one made trouble in the North –
    The Cocos tell the rest.
He sent a squadron to a coast
    Where treachery prevailed –
Gra'mercy! They were stricken hard
    On seas that Raleigh sailed!

"Now tell me what can England do?"
    Said the Kaiser to the Spy.
"Her ports are all unfortified
    And there your chances lie!"
He sent his ships to Scarborough,
    And called them back again.
The 'Blucher' lies in channel ooze
    With seven hundred men.

"Oh, tell me what can England do?"
  Said the Kaiser to the Spy.
"She can't hold Egypt for a day –
  (I have it from On High)."
And so the Kaiser paid the Turk
  To put the matter through –
And England's Queen of Egypt now,
  And boss of Turkey too.

"Now tell me what shall England do?"
  Said the Kaiser to the Spy.
You see that neither of them knew
  Much more than you or I.
But the blooming thing that's troubling me
  As the pregnant weeks to by,
Is wotinell shall England do
  When the Kaiser hangs that Spy!

Henry Lawson

Fighting Hard

"The Australians are fighting hard in Gallipoli." – *Cable*

*Rolling out to fight for England, singing songs across the
sea;*
*Rolling North to fight for England, and to fight for you
and me.*
*Fighting hard for France and England, where the storms
of Death are hurled;*
*Fighting hard for Australasia and the honour of the
World!*
   Fighting hard.

*Fighting hard for Sunny Queensland – fighting for
Bananaland,*
*Fighting hard for West Australia, and the mulga and the
sand;*
*Fighting hard for Plain and Wool-Track, and the haze of
western heat –*
*Fighting hard for South Australia and the bronze of
Farrar's Wheat!*
   Fighting hard.

Fighting hard for fair Victoria, and the mountain and the
  glen;
(And the Memory of Eureka — there were other tyrants
  then),
For the glorious Gippsland forests and the World's great
  Singing Star —
For the irrigation channels where the cabbage gardens
  are —
    Fighting hard.

Fighting hard for gale and earthquake, and the wind-
  swept ports between;
For the wild flax and manuka and the terraced hills of
  green.
Fighting hard for wooden homesteads, where the mighty
  kauris stand —
Fighting hard for fern and tussock! — fighting hard for
  Maoriland!
    Fighting hard.

Fighting hard for little Tassy, where the apple orchards
  grow;
(And the Northern Territory just to give the place a
  show),

*Fighting hard for Home and Empire, while the
    Commonwealth prevails –*
*And, in spite of all her blunders, dying hard for New
    South Wales.*
    Dying hard.

*Fighting for the Pride of Old Folk, and the people that
    you know;*
*And the girl you left behind you – (ah! the time is
    passing slow).*
*For the proud tears of a sister! come you back, or never
    come!*
*And the weary Elder Brother, looking after things at
    home –*
Fighting Hard! You Lucky Devils!
    Fighting hard.

E. W. Tennant

Home Thoughts in Laventie

Green gardens in Laventie!
Soldiers only know the street
Where the mud is churned and splashed about
By battle-wending feet;
And yet beside one stricken house there is a glimpse of
grass.
Look for it when you pass.

Beyond the church whose pitted spire
Seems balanced on a strand
Of swaying stone and tottering brick
Two roofless ruins stand,
And here behind the wreckage where the back wall should
have been
We found a garden green.

The grass was never trodden on,
The little path of gravel
Was overgrown with celandine,

No other folk did travel
along its weedy surface, but the nimble-footed mouse
    Running from house to house.

So all among the vivid blades
    Of soft and tender grass
    We lay, nor heard the limber wheels
    That pass and ever pass,
In noisy continuity until their very rattle
    Seems in itself a battle.

At length we rose up from this ease
    Of tranquil happy mind,
    And searched the garden's little length
    A fresh pleasaunce to find;
And there some yellow daffodils and jasmine hanging
    high
    Did rest the tired eye.

The fairest and most fragrant
    Of the many sweets we found,
Was a little bush of daphne flower
    Upon a grassy mound,

And so thick were the blossoms set and so divine the scent
  That we were well content.

  Hungry for spring, I bent my head,
    The perfume fanned my face,
And all my soul was dancing
    In that lovely little place,
Dancing with a measured step from wrecked and shattered
    towns
    Away upon the Downs.

  I saw green banks of daffodil,
    Slim poplars in the breeze,
Great tan-brown hares in gusty March
    A-courting on the leas;
And meadows with their glittering streams, and silver
    scurrying dace,
    Home — what a perfect place!

William Noel Hodgson

Ave, Mater – Atque Vale

The deathless mother, grey and battle-scarred,
Lies in the sanctuary of stately trees,
Where the deep Northern night is saffron starred
Above her head, and thro' the dusk she sees
God's shadowy fortress keep unsleeping guard.

From her full breast we drank of joy and mirth
And gave to her a boy's unreasoned heart,
Wherein Time's fullness was to bring to birth
Such passionate allegiance that to part
Seemed like the passing of all light on earth.

Now on the threshold of a man's estate,
With a new depth of love akin to pain
I ask thy blessing, while I dedicate
My life and sword, with promise to maintain
Thine ancient honour yet inviolate.

Last night dream-hearted in the Abbey's spell
We stood to sing old Simeon's passing hymn,
When sudden splendour of the sunset fell
Full on my eyes, and passed and left all dim —
At once a summons and a deep farewell.

I am content — our life is but a trust
From the great hand of God, and if I keep
The immortal Treasure clean of mortal rust
Against His claim, 'tis well, and let me sleep
Among the not dishonourable dust.

John Freeman

Happy is England Now

There is not anything more wonderful
Than a great people moving towards the deep
Of an unguessed and unfeared future; nor
Is aught so dear of all held dear before
As the new passion stirring in their veins
When the destroying Dragon wakes from sleep.

Happy is England now, as never yet!
And though the sorrows of the slow days fret
Her faithfullest children, grief itself is proud.
Ev'n the warm beauty of this spring and summer
That turns to bitterness turns then to gladness,
Since for this England the beloved ones died.

Happy is England in the brave that die
For wrongs not hers and wrongs so sternly hers;
Happy in those that give, give, and endure
The pain that never the new years may cure;
Happy in all her dark woods, green fields, towns,
Her hills and rivers and her chafing sea.

Whate'er was dear before is dearer now.
There's not a bird singing upon his bough
But sings the sweeter in our English ears:
There's not a nobleness of heart, hand, brain
But shines the purer; happiest is England now
In those that fight, and watch with pride and tears.

GEORGE ROBERT SIMS

WON'T YOU JOIN THE ARMY?

*When the fairies are not dancing in the moonlit glade and
 dell,*
*They are busy putting mortals underneath their fairy
 spell,*
*And a fairy boy who wanders o 'er a world at work and
 play*
*Longs to put the boys of Britain 'neath his fairy spell
 today.*
*'Neath the spell of England's honour one who's British
 born himself*
*Wants to hold you, for I've told you Puck's a little
 English elf,*
*He is going to fight for England and he wants you ev'ry
 one*
To join the little Army that is out against the Hun.
    Won't you join the Army? Won't you come with me?
    *Won't you come with me, boys, to Berlin on the
 Spree?*
    Say goodbye to Kate or Nan,
    She'll be proud that you're a man.

Won't you, won't you, won't you come? Won't
  you, won't you come and join?
Won't you, won't you, won't you, won't you
  come and join with me?

Of all the gallant deeds you've done, we've heard in
  Fairyland,
We know that ne'er a foe of old your valour could
  withstand.
But now there's danger on the sea and danger on the
  shore,
That Britain in her island pride has never known before.
The Land that no invader's foot has trod since Harold's
  day
Is threaten'd by a foreign horde who helpless women slay!
Then up for women, bairns and home, ye men of British
  blood,
To pluck the German eagle's crest and dam the German
  flood.
  Won't you join the Army? Won't you come with me?
  Won't you rally round the flag across the
    Northern Sea?
  Say goodbye to Kate or Nan,

She'll be proud that you're a man.

Won't you, won't you, won't you come? Won't you,
    won't you come and join?

Won't you, won't you, won't you, won't you come
    and join with me?

J.R. WREFORD

LORD, WHILE FOR ALL MANKIND WE PRAY

Lord, while for all mankind we pray
Of every clime and coast,
O hear us for our native land,
The land we love the most.

O guard our shores from every foe;
With peace our borders bless;
With prosperous times our cities crown,
Our fields with plenteousness.

Unite us in the sacred love
Of knowledge, truth, and thee;
And let our hills and valleys shout
The songs of liberty.

Lord of the nations, thus to thee
Our country we commend;
Be thou her refuge and her trust,
Her everlasting friend.

RUPERT BROOKE

THE SOLDIER

If I should die, think only this of me:
  That there's some corner of a foreign field
That is for ever England. There shall be
  In that rich earth a richer dust concealed;
A dust whom England bore, shaped, made aware,
  Gave, once, her flower to love, her ways to roam,
A body of England's, breathing English air,
  Washed by the rivers blest by suns of home.

And think, this heart, all evil shed away,
  A pulse in the eternal mind, no less
    Gives somewhere back the thoughts by England
      given;
Her sights and sounds; dreams happy as her day;
  And laughter, learnt of friends; and gentleness,
    In hearts at peace, under an English heaven.

LAURENCE BINYON

FOR THE FALLEN

With proud thanksgiving, a mother for her children,
England mourns for her dead across the sea.
Flesh of her flesh they were, spirit of her spirit,
Fallen in the cause of the free.

Solemn the drums thrill: Death august and royal
Sings sorrow up into immortal spheres.
There is music in the midst of desolation
And a glory that shines upon our tears.

They went with songs to the battle, they were young,
Straight of limb, true of eye, steady and aglow.
They were staunch to the end against odds uncounted.
They fell with their faces to the foe.

They shall grow not old, as we that are left grow old:
Age shall not weary them, nor the years condemn.
At the going down of the sun and in the morning
We will remember them.

They mingle not with their laughing comrades again;
They sit no more at familiar tables of home;
They have no lot in our labour of the day-time;
They sleep beyond England's foam.

But where our desires are and our hopes profound,
Felt as a well-spring that is hidden from sight,
To the innermost heart of their own land they are known
As the stars are known to the Night;

As the stars that shall be bright when we are dust,
Moving in marches upon the heavenly plain,
As the stars that are starry in the time of our darkness,
To the end, to the end, they remain.

WILLIAM BLAKE

JERUSALEM

And did those feet in ancient time
Walk upon England's mountains green?
And was the holy Lamb of God
On England's pleasant pastures seen?

And did the Countenance Divine
Shine forth upon our clouded hills?
And was Jerusalem builded here
Among these dark Satanic Mills?

Bring me my Bow of burning gold:
Bring me my Arrows of desire:
Bring me my Spear: O clouds unfold!
Bring me my Chariot of fire.

I will not cease from Mental Fight,
Nor shall my Sword sleep in my hand
Till we have built Jerusalem
In England's green and pleasant Land.

ROBERT BROWNING

HOME THOUGHTS, FROM ABROAD

Oh, to be in England
Now that April's there,
And whoever wakes in England
Sees, some morning, unaware,
That the lowest boughs and the brush-wood sheaf
Round the elm-tree bole are in tiny leaf,
While the chaffinch sings on the orchard bough
In England – now!

And after April, when May follows,
And the whitethroat builds, and all the swallows –
Hark! where my blossomed pear-tree in the hedge
Leans to the field and scatters on the clover
Blossoms and dewdrops – at the bent-spray's edge –
That's the wise thrush; he sings each song twice over,
Lest you should think he never could recapture
The first fine careless rapture!
And though the fields look rough with hoary dew,
All will be gay when noontide wakes anew
The buttercups, the little children's dower,
– Far brighter than this gaudy melon-flower!

ROBERT BROWNING

HOME THOUGHTS, FROM THE SEA

Nobly, nobly Cape Saint Vincent to the north-west died
    away;
Sunset, ran, one glorious blood-red, reeking into Cadiz
    Bay;
Bluish 'mid the burning water, full in face Trafalgar lay;
In the dimmest north-east distance, dawned Gibraltar
    grand and grey;
"Here and here did England help me, – how can I help
    England?" – say,
Whoso turns as I, this evening, turn to God to praise and
    pray,
While Jove's planet rises yonder, silent over Africa.

Sir Cecil Spring-Rice

The Two Fatherlands

I vow to thee, my country, all earthly things above,
Entire and whole and perfect, the service of my love;
The love that asks no question, the love that stands the
    test,
That lays upon the altar the dearest and the best;
The love that never falters, the love that pays the price,
The love that makes undaunted the final sacrifice.

And there's another country, I've heard of long ago,
Most dear to them that love her, most great to them that
    know;
We may not count her armies, we may not see her King;
Her fortress is a faithful heart, her pride is suffering;
And soul by soul and silently her shining bounds
    increase,
And her ways are ways of gentleness and all her paths are
    peace.

WILLIAM HENLEY

ENGLAND, MY ENGLAND

What have I done for you,
England, my England?
What is there I would not do,
England, my own?
With your glorious eyes austere,
As the Lord were walking near,
Whisp'ring terrible things and dear
As the Song on your bugles blown,
England, England,
Round the world on your bugles blown!

Where shall the watchful Sun,
England, my England,
Match the masterwork you've done,
England, my own?
When shall he rejoice agen
Such a breed of mighty men
As come forward, one to ten,
To the Song on your bugles blown,
England, England,
Down the years on your bugles blown?

Ever the faith endures,
England, my England:
"Take and break us: we are yours,
England, my own!
Life is good, and joy runs high
Between English earth and sky;
Death is death; but we shall die
To the Song on your bugles blown,
England, England,
To the stars on your bugles blown!"

They call you proud and hard,
England, my England:
You with worlds to watch and ward,
England, my own!
You whose mailed hand keeps the keys
Of such teeming destinies
You could know nor dread nor ease
Were the Song on your bugles blown,
England, England,
Round the Pit on your bugles blown!

Mother of Ships whose might,
England, my England,
Is the fierce old Sea's delight,
England, my own,
Chosen daughter of the Lord,
Spouse-in-Chief of the ancient sword,
There's the menace of the Word
In the Song on your bugles blown,
England, England,
Out of heaven on your bugles blown!

Rudyard Kipling

Land of our Birth ...

Land of our birth, we pledge to thee
Our love and toil in the years to be;
When we are grown and take our place
As men and women with our race.

Father in heaven who lovest all,
O help thy children when they call,
That they may build from age to age
An undefilèd heritage.

Teach us to bear the yoke in youth,
With steadfastness and careful truth;
That in our time thy grace may give
The truth whereby the nations live.

Teach us to rule ourselves alway,
Controlled and cleanly night and day;
That we may bring, if need arise,
No maimed or worthless sacrifice.

Teach us to look in all our ends
On thee for judge, and not our friends;
That we, with thee, may walk uncowed
By fear or favour of the crowd.

Teach us the strength that cannot seek.
By deed or thought, to hurt the weak;
That, under thee, we may possess
Man's strength to comfort man's distress.

Teach us delight in simple things,
And mirth that has no bitter springs;
Forgiveness free of evil done,
And love to all men 'neath the sun.

Land of our birth, our faith, our pride,
For whose dear sake our fathers died;
O Motherland, we pledge to thee,
Head, heart, and hand through the years to
    be!

Fred E. Weatherly

Up From Somerset

Oh, we came up from Somerset,
To see the Great Review;
There was Mary drest in her Sunday best,
And our boy Billee too.
The drums were rolling rub-a-dub,
The trumpets tootled too,
When right up rode His Majesty,
An' says "An who be you?"

"Oh, we'm come up from Somerset,
Where the cider apples grow,
We'm come to see your Majesty,
An' how the world do go.
And when you're wanting anyone,
If you'll kindly let us know,
We'll all come up from Somerset,
Because we loves you so!"

Then the Queen she look'd at Mary,
"An' what's your name?" she said,
But Mary blush'd like any rose,
An' hung her pretty head.
So I ups and nudges Mary,
"Speak up and tell her, do!"
So she said "If it please, your Majesty,
My name is Mary too!

An we'm come up from Somerset,
Where the cider apples grow,
Where the gals can hem an' sew an' stitch,
And also reap and hoe,
An' if you're wanting any gals,
An' will kindly let us know,
We'll all come from Somerset,
Because we loves you so!"

Then the King look'd down at Billee-boy,
Before they rode away,
"An' what is he going for to be?"
His Majesty did say.
So Billee pull'd his forelock,
And stood up trim and true,

"Oh, I'm going to be a soldier, Sir
For I wants to fight for you!

For we'm come up from Somerset,
Where the cider apples grow,
For we're all King's men in Somerset,
As they were long, long ago,
An' when you're wanting soldier boys,
An' there's fighting for to do,
You just send word to Somerset,
An' we'll all be up for you!"

Neil Munro

To Exiles

Are you not weary in your distant places,
Far, far from Scotland of the mist and storm,
In drowsy airs, the sun-smite on your faces,
The days so long and warm?
When all around you lie the strange fields sleeping,
The dreary woods where no fond memories roam,
Do not your sad hearts over seas come leaping
To the highlands and the lowlands of your Home?

Wild cries the Winter, loud through all our valleys;
The midnights roar, the grey noons echo back;
Round steep storm-bitten coasts the eager galleys
Beat for kind harbours from horizons black;
We tread the miry roads, the rain-drenched heather,
We are the men, we battle, we endure!
God's pity for you people in your weather
Of swooning winds, calm seas, and skies demure!

Wild cries the Winter, and we walk song-haunted
Over the moors and by the thundering falls,
Or where the dirge of a brave past is chaunted
In dolorous dusks by immemorial walls.
Though rains may thrash on us, the great mists blind
  us,
And lightning rend the pine-tree on the hill,
Yet are we strong, yet shall the morning find us
Children of tempest all unshaken still.

We wander where the little grey towns cluster
Deep in the hills, or selvedging the sea,
By farm-lands lone, by woods were wildfowl muster
To shelter from the day's inclemency;
And night will come, and then far through the
  darkling,
A light will shine out in the sounding glen,
And it will mind us of some fond eye's sparkling,
And we'll be happy then.

Let torrents pour then, let the great winds rally,
Snow-silence fall or lightning blast the pine;
That light of Home shines warmly in the valley,
And, exiled son of Scotland, it is thine.

Far have you wandered over seas of longing,
And now you drowse, and now you well may weep,
When all the recollections come a-thronging
Of this rude country where your fathers sleep.

They sleep, but still the hearth is warmly glowing,
While the wild Winter blusters round their land;
That light of Home, the wind so bitter blowing –
Do they not haunt your dreams on alien Strand?
Love, strength, and tempest – oh, come back and
    share them!
Here's the old cottage, here the open door;
Fond are our hearts although we do not bare them, –
They're yours, and you are ours for evermore.

JOHN DRINKWATER

THE MIDLANDS

Black in the summer night my Cotswold hill
    Aslant my window sleeps, beneath a sky
Deep as the bedded violets that fill
    March woods with dusky passion. As I lie
Abed between cool walls I watch the host
    Of the slow stars lit over Gloucester plain,
And drowsily the habit of these most
    Beloved of English lands moves in my brain,
While silence holds dominion of the dark,
Save when the foxes from the spinneys bark.

I see the valleys in their morning mist
    Wreathed under limpid hills in moving light,
Happy with many a yeoman melodist:
    I see the little roads of twinkling white
Busy with fieldward teams and market gear
    Of rosy men, cloth-gaitered, who can tell
The many-minded changes of the year,
    Who know why crops and kine fare ill or well;
I see the sun persuade the mist away,
Till town and stead are shining to the day.

I see the wagons move along the rows
    Of ripe and summer-breathing clover-flower,
I see the lissom husbandman who knows
    Deep in his heart the beauty of his power,
As, lithely pitched, the full-heaped fork bids on
    The harvest home. I hear the rickyard fill
With gossip as in generations gone,
    While wagon follows wagon from the hill.
I think how, when our seasons all are sealed,
Shall come the unchanging harvest from the field.

I see the barns and comely manors planned
    By men who somehow moved in comely thought,
Who, with a simple shippon to their hand,
    As men upon some godlike business wrought;
I see the little cottages that keep
    Their beauty still where since Plantagenet
Have come the shepherds happily to sleep,
    Finding the loves and cups of cider set;
I see the twisted shepherds, brown and old,
Driving at dusk their glimmering sheep to fold.

And now the valleys that upon the sun
    Broke from their opal veils are veiled again,

And the last light upon the wolds is done,
*   And silence falls on flocks and fields and men;*
And black upon the night I watch my hill,
*   And the stars shine, and there an owly wing*
Brushes the night, and all again is still,
*   And, from this land of worship that I sing,*
I turn to sleep, content that from my sires
I draw the blood of England's midmost shires.

ARTHUR BENSON

LAND OF HOPE AND GLORY

Dear Land of Hope, thy hope is crowned,
God make thee mightier yet!
On Sov'ran brows, beloved, renowned,
Once more thy crown is set.
Thine equal laws, by Freedom gained,
Have ruled thee well and long;
By Freedom gained, by Truth maintained,
Thine Empire shall be strong.

> *Land of Hope and Glory,*
> *Mother of the Free,*
> *How shall we extol thee,*
> *Who are born of thee?*
> *Wider still and wider shall thy bounds be set;*
> *God, who made thee mighty, make thee mightier yet;*
> *God, who made thee mighty, make thee mightier yet.*

Thy fame is ancient as the days,
As Ocean large and wide;
A pride that dares, and heeds not praise,
A stem and silent pride;

Not that false joy that dreams content
With what our sires have won;
The blood a hero sire hath spent
Still nerves a hero son.

   Land of Hope and Glory,
   Mother of the Free,
   How shall we extol thee,
   Who are born of thee?
   Wider still and wider shall thy bounds be set;
   God, who made thee mighty, make thee mightier yet;
   God, who made thee mighty, make thee mightier yet.